Turning Over the Leaf

by WG Stillwater

kelley creative

TURNING OVER THE LEAF

BY WG STILLWATER

ISBN 978-1-7331088-2-9

Published by Kelley Creative.

Cover and book design by Kelley Creative.
www.kelleycreative.design

Contents

Introduction

Turning Over the Leaf is a journey about facing challenges in life and not letting fears hold you back from pursuing your dreams. This story is based on true events that have led to me pursuing my own dreams and passions in life. Through my own struggles and challenges, my hope is to help inspire those who may need a hand in getting back up and trying again. If you feel inspired by reading this story, try to pass on the positivity to someone else and soon you will see just how much influence you have in creating the world you wish to see. Thank you for reading Turning Over the Leaf and I hope you all continue chasing your dreams.

CHAPTER 1

Shattered Glass

When we come to a crossroads in life and choose to follow our dreams, that's when we really begin to live.

Sometimes you make bad decisions and your whole world comes crashing down right before your eyes. The boat that had kept you afloat takes on water, and fast. It might be sinking, but luckily you still have some choices to make. You can go down with the ship, swim back to safety, or fix the leak and continue chasing your dreams.

Which choice would you make?

I'd always kept a positive outlook on life. My glass was half full. Then, one day I found myself in a situation where I knocked over my glass. I tried to save it, but I wasn't quick enough. The water spilled out all over the table. Just when I thought things couldn't get any worse, my glass rolled off the edge of the table and smashed onto the floor.

Now my glass was broken and there was water everywhere. While I was cleaning up the mess, I saw my reflection in some of the broken glass. Seeing all of those broken pieces lying everywhere reminded me of the poor decision that had recently shattered my life.

I had thought my life was going pretty well up to that point. I had a roof over my head and a steady job, and the bills were getting paid. My friends were doing okay and I had a family to come home to. Then my whole life changed because of a series of events that led to me making a bad decision.

I started replaying the incident in my mind and asking myself, "What did I just do?"

I had created the mess that I was in, but I wasn't sure if I could clean it up this time. When I made mistakes in the past, I was always able to correct them and move on. Now it felt like everyone was judging me for my poor decision.

I thought to myself, "That's not me. I'm not the monster they say I am."

I started losing my positive outlook on life.

Had I just been living in a dream, and reality had finally struck? Was I too trusting of the world in giving it the benefit of the doubt?

Then I started to question everything in my life—the decisions I'd made, the relationships I'd had and the jobs I'd worked.

I thought, "Is this really what life is about? Just go to work, pay the bills and get no reward for the hard work? Just a death certificate and another bill to pay?" Then I thought about all the chaos going on in the world that seemed to be getting crazier by the day.

I was going down the path of feeling like life just wasn't worth it anymore. If nobody else cared about the world, then why should I?

I eventually cleaned up the mess and went to get another glass. But when I opened the cabinet door, the only thing I saw was a paper cup. I looked everywhere for another glass, but it turned out that I had broken the last one. I really didn't want to use the paper cup, but it was all I had left, so I grabbed a hold of it.

I opened the refrigerator to fill up my cup, but there wasn't any water. Then I went over to the sink and turned on the faucet, but nothing came out. I proceeded to check every faucet in the house, but there still wasn't any water.

Not only had I broken my glass, but I didn't have water, either.

There were no signs of water anywhere, and I was slowly beginning to lose hope. I had always helped out others if I could, but this time I was the one who needed some help. Sure, my family and friends were supportive, but I didn't want to burden them with my mistake.

So after days and days with no water, I finally decided that I needed to look for water somewhere else.

CHAPTER 2

Spring Forward

It was the first day of spring and the trees were starting to bounce back up full of life again. I thought this was a great time to start my quest.

"Surely there is water out there somewhere," I told myself. "I just need to find it for myself."

I didn't know which way to go at first, so I kept watching for a sign to point me in the right direction. Just then I looked across a field and noticed a huge maple tree sparkling in the sun. I was amazed by all the wonderful branches sprouting out everywhere, so I walked over to get a closer look.

As I was appreciating the tree, a beautiful leaf caught my attention.

I moved a little closer to the leaf, and the tree spoke to me. "You don't have to go on this journey alone. Take this leaf with you. If you get lost along the way, just hold it up in the air. When the wind blows it away, follow it to find your way."

When I heard the tree speak, I thought I was imagining things. Then the leaf slowly drifted into my hands and I was convinced it was the sign I was looking for. So I thanked the tree, put the leaf in my bag, and headed on my way.

I must have walked for miles, but there were still no signs of water. The path I was walking on wasn't very clear and there were many trees blocking my way. I kept trying to get through the overgrown trees, but some of the branches were just too big to get past. After a few more unsuccessful attempts, I took a break to consider my options.

That's when I remembered the leaf in my bag. So I took it out, held it up in the air, and waited for a sign. But nothing happened. I still had the leaf in the air when I felt a buzz by my ear.

I quickly turned and I saw a hummingbird hovering above me. I remained still and didn't make a sound. The hummingbird flew a little closer to the leaf in my hand and just hovered there, looking into my eyes.

I was amazed by how beautiful the hummingbird was and then I heard it say, "Sometimes your journey can be met with great resistance. With so many barriers blocking your path, it's easy to give up and quit. That's when you need a little guidance to help you see that there is another path."

Then the hummingbird flew toward a huge patch of overgrown bushes and hovered above them.

I asked myself, "Is that the path the hummingbird wants me to take?" I had thought about following that route earlier, but there were just too many bushes over there. The path was so overgrown I didn't think I could make it through. I didn't even have anything to cut through them, much less make a path.

I thought about what the hummingbird said. Then I saw it fly up a little farther and out of my sight. I walked over to the bushes to check it out, and it was just as I thought: It was overgrown with bushes and weeds, and there were vines growing everywhere. Getting through the path was going to take a miracle.

I looked a little farther ahead and saw there was a clear field just past all the bushes.

I thought maybe the hummingbird was right about going this way. If I was able to successfully navigate my way through all the weeds, I just might be able to create my own path and make it out on the other side. So I took a leap of faith and started walking through the bushes.

While I was fighting my way through the shrubs, I felt something scratch my leg. I looked down to see thorny vines slicing through my pants. I tried stepping around the vines, but there were just too many. So I kept going through them. My pants were getting torn and I was getting tired, so I took a break for a moment.

While I was standing there I contemplated turning back because the route didn't look promising. To my surprise I saw the hummingbird flying toward me again. I still had the leaf with me so I held it up in the air.

The hummingbird landed on the leaf and spoke to me again. "Looks like you have some choices to make. You can stop right here and see what happens. You can go back to where you came from and return to safety. Or you can keep pushing forward and continue on your journey. Your future is unknown, but you've already seen your past. The choice is yours to make."

I thought about those words and what they meant to me. I didn't want to go back to the same old situation that I had come from. Besides, I had set out on a journey to find some water and I wasn't about to give up just yet. I refocused to get my mind right and then geared myself up to continue going forward.

As I continued my way through the bushes, I still had to get through several vines that were impeding my progress. I was stuck again, so I bent down to clear the vines from my feet. That was when I noticed it wasn't the vines holding me back. I looked down again and saw snakes all around me, and I instantly felt fear.

Immediately I froze. I was terrified of snakes and now I was stuck in a situation where I couldn't move.

"Out of all things, why did it have to be snakes?" I asked myself.

I looked at the snakes again and realized that I had to face them if I wanted to move forward. So I gathered up enough courage and started walking around them. A few tried to strike my legs, but I was quick enough to dodge them. I evaded a few more, only to find that I had to deal with several others. The snakes seemed to be multiplying the farther I made it past them. At one point I tripped trying to avoid one snake, only to fall and find myself face to face with another one.

There I was, facing the head of a snake and wondering if I had made a mistake coming this way. I briefly thought about giving up and just letting the snake strike me—then all my worries could have been over. But I thought about the journey that I was on.

I said to myself, "Not today. I'm not going to let my fears keep me from moving on."

I grabbed the snake around the neck and looked at it. I could easily have killed it if I'd wanted to. Just then I thought of something. I decided to show mercy and threw the snake in the direction of the other snakes in front of me. To my surprise, the snake started fighting with the others. This was exactly the diversion I needed. While the snakes were fighting, I seized the opportunity and ran as fast as I could to get past them.

That day I ran the fastest I think I've ever run in my life, and I didn't stop until I made it into the clear. There was so much open space in front of me, I just lay down in the grass looking up into the sky, feeling relieved.

I asked myself, "With so much open space, where do I go from here?"

Although I wasn't sure, I knew exactly how to find out. I stood up, took out the leaf, and held it up again.

I waited for a few minutes, wondering if I was on my own. Then the hummingbird came flying toward me. I was really beginning to like this hummingbird, so I just waited to see if it had another message for me.

It landed on the leaf and spoke to me again.

"Facing your fears can be a huge step in life. Some will never even try and will stay put. Some will keep moving forward and win. Some will lose, falling flat on their face. Sometimes the toughest part is getting back up and trying again."

Just then the hummingbird flew into the open field and off to the right.

CHAPTER 3

Mechanical Parts

I couldn't get what the hummingbird said out of my mind. Then I compared it to my own life. It was beginning to feel like I was on more than just a quest for water. I trusted in the guidance that I was getting, so I walked through the field in the direction that the hummingbird had flown.

Once I got to the other side of the field, I came to a path that led through the woods. This time the path was a little more defined, so I continued down it, hoping that it led to water somewhere. After a few miles of walking, I didn't see any signs of water anywhere, but I felt at ease knowing that I still had the leaf with me.

I came to a clearing on the path where a few people were gathered around talking to each other. I stopped to listen and was drawn into some of the stories of their journeys.

One person in particular was talking about turning a negative situation into a positive one. I liked listening to his story, and he seemed to have a positive attitude like mine. So when he finished his story, I went up to him and asked if he could point me in the right direction to find some water. I described my situation and found out that he was looking for water as well.

He said, "I'm a mechanic and I love fixing things, but I need fixing myself."

I thought about the journey I was on and thought to myself, "I could use all the help I can get." So I suggested to the mechanic that he come along with me.

He walked away and I thought he was declining my invitation. But instead, he grabbed his backpack and quickly walked back over to me.

He said he would be happy to help and that the best place to find water would be in the river. He didn't quite know how to get to the river himself, but he decided to join me to see if we could find it together.

We walked down the path for what seemed like hours, but there were no signs of the river anywhere. So I asked the mechanic if we were on the right path. He wasn't sure if the path led to the river, but he assured me that if we kept the faith, good things would come.

So we continued on our way, and I kept the faith just as he suggested. While we were walking I talked about how I was questioning everything in my life and that I was beginning to lose hope.

The mechanic said that he had lots of questions himself, but he always tried to have faith that things would get better. "I didn't panic when bad things happened in my past," he explained. "Somehow I always managed to turn things around for the better." He stressed to me again the importance of keeping the faith.

I took his words to heart and slowly started to feel a little hope returning.

After clearing a few obstacles on the path, we came upon a crossroads where the path went in two different directions. We stopped to consider the two paths and where they might lead. We contemplated splitting up and taking separate paths, but so far we seemed to be helping each other. Just then I remembered the leaf in my bag. So I took it out and held it up in the air to see if it could point us in the right direction.

The mechanic saw the leaf and asked me where I got it. I told him the story behind the leaf, and now we were both focused on seeing what was going to happen.

I held the leaf back up and asked it which path was the right one to take.

I wasn't sure what to expect. But then the hummingbird came flying toward us and landed on the leaf.

It looked at both of us and paused a moment.

I saw from the look in the mechanic's eyes that he was totally focused on the hummingbird. I could tell he was appreciating the beautiful bird just like I was. Then the hummingbird spoke to us.

"Sometimes we need a little guidance in life to point us in the right direction. We all get lost sometimes, so don't be afraid to ask for help. If you're lost or confused, you don't have to continue going down the wrong path. There are many different paths that can lead to your destination. You just have to decide which path is the right one for you. Look within yourselves first and then look at the two paths again. Deep down you will know which one to take."

The mechanic had a shocked look on his face, and then the hummingbird flew away.

We thought about what the hummingbird said, but we still weren't sure which path to take. Just then the wind blew the leaf to the path on the left.

I asked the mechanic which path he was thinking about taking, and he said the path on the left.

I told him that I was thinking about taking the same path, so we trusted our instincts and headed down the path on the left.

As we walked a little farther, I noticed the temperature was dropping and there were a lot of rocks all over the ground. We didn't let the rocks deter us, though, and we were able to adjust to the rocky terrain.

As we came to a clearing in the trees, the mechanic pointed out that he could hear some water flowing up ahead of us. We ran up closer to get a look. It was definitely water, but unfortunately there were some large trees blocking our view. There was also a very steep drop down a hill to the water. If we wanted to get down to it, it was going to take teamwork to make it.

I asked the mechanic if that was the river, but he wasn't sure. He said it would be worth checking out.

I looked down the rocky hill and then back at the mechanic. He just smiled and said, "It's going to be a challenge, but I think we can both make it down okay."

I was thinking, "There is no way we can make it down the hill. Is he crazy?"

I looked down the hill again and my fear of heights was not helping my nerves at all, but the mechanic was right. If we made it down the hill, we would at last find the water we'd been searching for.

The mechanic pulled out a hammer from his backpack and handed it to me. Then he pulled out another one for himself.

I looked at the claw hammer and asked, "What else do you have in your backpack?"

He smiled and said that he had what he needed, then he swung the hammer into the dirt. He thought it was safe enough to try and then started backing down the hill. He made it about fifteen feet and was making pretty good progress, so I decided to give it a try.

I thought to myself, "Okay, here goes nothing." And I started backing down the hill like the mechanic was.

I used the claw end of the hammer to steady my descent down the hill. A few times the smaller rocks would give out, but I had a pretty good grip on the ground and was able to keep pace with the mechanic. I kept looking down to gauge how far we still had to go when suddenly the rocks gave out from under me. I lost my footing and started sliding down the hill. The mechanic reacted quickly by grabbing my arm to stop me from

sliding farther. I regained my footing and we both took a break for a moment to catch our breath.

The mechanic looked down and just smiled.

I looked down and asked him why he was smiling.

He said, "You gave me a great idea. By slipping and sliding, I think we can both get the rest of the way down the hill."

I was already thinking he was a little crazy, but this was even crazier.

Without hesitation, the mechanic started sliding down the hill on his backside. I watched him make it to the bottom safely without a hitch.

I thought, "He's crazy and a little reckless too," but I was starting to like his kind of crazy.

So I gathered up enough courage and started sliding down the hill. Unfortunately, I took a tumble and started rolling down the hill. As I was rolling I felt my jacket come off. My bag was getting torn up as well. But I finally made it to the bottom of the hill with just a few bumps and bruises.

I looked up the hill and saw my jacket, but I wasn't about to go back up to get it.

The mechanic came over to help me up and asked if I had fun sliding down the hill.

I brushed off some dirt and started laughing because it had been kind of exciting.

He laughed and said that this was another situation that sort of worked itself out for the better.

I agreed and said, "Turning a negative into a positive, right?"

He nodded in agreement and smiled.

We took a moment to regroup and then looked through the trees ahead of us. There was definitely water flowing on the other side of them, so we quickly walked through to check it out.

"Finally," I thought to myself "we found some water."

Turning Over the Leaf

Walking down to the creek felt like an accomplishment. As we neared the water, I opened my bag and saw that it was pretty torn up. I checked on the leaf and was relieved to find that it was still perfectly intact. So I took out my last paper cup and dipped it into the creek to get some water. When I lifted it up, the bottom fell out. When I saw the water dripping out of the bottom of the cup, I just shook my head in disgust. I had finally found some water, but now I didn't have a cup to fill up.

The mechanic saw my paper cup and said, "We don't need cups."

Then he dipped his hands into the creek and took a sip of water.

So I cupped my hands under the water and slowly took a sip. It was cool and tasted so fresh. Even though I didn't have a cup to drink from, it was still rewarding.

The mechanic said that the water was great, but it wasn't anything like the river. The creek had limits, but the river offered more of a chance to fulfill our journey.

I thought about what the mechanic said and then thought about our journey. Sure, we found some water, but if we were able to find the river, the possibilities could be endless. Then I started thinking of a way to continue on the path that we were already on. We had just slid down a very steep hill, so going back up wasn't an option. After some discussions about which way to proceed, I took out the leaf to see if it could guide us in the right direction.

I held it up, but nothing happened. I thought maybe we were too far away from the hummingbird. There was very little wind and the leaf wasn't moving at all. Then, to my surprise, the hummingbird came flying up toward us.

The mechanic and I were both relieved to see it, and we waited to see if it had a message for us.

The hummingbird hovered in front of us, then landed on the leaf and spoke to us again.

"Embarking on a journey can be frightening at times, but it can be very enlightening as well. You can discover some

great qualities about yourself and conquer some fears along the way. There may be ups and downs, but if you can find a way to balance out the two, you can move forward without fear holding you back."

Just then, the hummingbird flew straight toward the end of the creek.

I took another mental note of what the hummingbird said, then I looked at the mechanic.

He chuckled and said, "I'm really beginning to like this hummingbird."

I laughed because that was exactly how I felt.

Chapter 4

Biker Trails

We followed the hummingbird to the end of the creek, where I saw a road just past the rocks. I looked a little farther ahead and saw that the road went slightly uphill.

I thought, "We both just slid down the hill earlier, and now it looks like we are going to have to walk back up it."

We agreed that it had to be the direction the hummingbird wanted us to go in, so we started walking toward the road. As we approached it, we noticed there was a steady incline. But it was gradual, so we started walking up the road.

We walked for a few miles; from time to time we would take a break to catch our breath. At one point we came upon a man who was looking at his broken-down bike. We decided to help him because this was right up the mechanic's alley. The mechanic took off his backpack and laid out some tools that he needed. I was amazed by how organized he was and how many tools he had.

The mechanic explained, "I never know when I'll need them, but I carry them with me just in case."

He worked fast, and it seemed he'd fixed the man's bike within minutes. The man was amazed by how little time the repair took. Then we all shook hands.

I explained our journey to the biker, and we found out that he was also searching for water. After listening to his story about always wanting to help people, we asked him to come along with us.

The biker said that he didn't like groups and was better off going on his own.

The mechanic and I kept trying to convince him to come along, insisting that we could use his help. The biker didn't think the river was on the path we were on, but he finally decided to join us.

So the three of us continued on the path, hoping to find the river. We listened to the biker's story as we walked. He explained that he had been through some tough struggles in his life, but he was working his way back to finding himself. We learned that he was willing to help people, and doing so helped him feel like he was making a difference in people's lives.

After we told him about our own struggles, he was glad that he had come along to help us. We all exchanged more stories from our pasts and now we were even more determined to find the river.

As we got a little farther up the road, it looked like there was a storm brewing above us. We dismissed it as nothing major when it started to sprinkle, but then the rain picked up and soon there was a downpour. Now we had to decide whether to continue walking or weather the storm.

The mechanic pointed out a cave where we could take cover, so we ran over to it to wait out the storm. While we were waiting we saw a van that appeared to be stuck in the mud. As we looked a little closer we noticed that the van was sliding and getting closer to the edge of a cliff.

The biker saw the dilemma and, without warning, darted off on his bike to help. The rain picked up and was coming down in buckets. We couldn't see very well through the storm, but I did see that the biker had fallen off his bike.

The mechanic and I ran up the road to help him, as he and his bike were about to go sliding off the cliff. We reached down, grabbed his shoulders, and helped him to his feet. As we pulled him up, his bike fell over the cliff. We heard a crash when it hit bottom.

The biker didn't care about his bike, and without hesitation he was ready to help the people in the van.

It looked like they were scared and didn't know what to do. The driver was pushing the gas pedal to keep the van from sliding, but that just made the van slide even more.

The biker devised a plan to help them. He told us to grab a huge tree that was lying on the ground. Then we all three dragged it over and stuck it behind the van to keep it from sliding. Now all we had to do was create traction so the van could get going back uphill.

The mechanic pointed out a few more tree branches, so we gathered some up and stuck them behind the van's tires.

The mechanic told the driver to punch the gas again. The van sprung out of the hole and back onto the road.

By following the biker's plan to a T, we were able to work together to free the van from the mud. The people in the van thanked us and offered to give us some money for helping them. We declined their offer, though, because the journey wasn't about money. We had more important goals, and helping them was the least we could do. The people thanked us again and gave us some sandwiches before they drove off.

I looked up into the rainy sky and thought to myself, "Maybe there is still good in this world after all."

Helping out those people in need reminded me of the goodness in people. We may have sacrificed our own safety in assisting them, but it felt like the right thing to do.

I looked up into the sky again and the rain suddenly stopped. My faith in humanity was slowly returning, and I had the mechanic and biker to thank for it.

We walked back to the edge of the cliff to see what had happened to the bike. We could see it was smashed all over the rocks at the bottom.

The biker said, "Maybe it's time that I got a car instead."

We all laughed for a moment and the biker thanked us for helping. The mechanic and I were just glad that he hadn't gone over the cliff with his bike. We all hugged it out and thanked each other.

After a break, we walked back to the cave to rest up before continuing up the road. We talked more about our journey and how we were all helping each other heal from our past mistakes. The biker and the mechanic ate their sandwiches while we talked about our goals in life. I wasn't that hungry, so I put my sandwich in my bag for later.

After about thirty minutes we were re-energized, so we continued on our journey to find the river. The road finally leveled off some shortly before we came upon another crossroads—only this time there were three paths to choose from.

The mechanic suggested that I use the leaf again to help guide us on the right path.

The biker wondered what we were talking about, so we explained the story behind the leaf. He was a little skeptical and wasn't sure he believed our story. To this point the leaf seemed to be guiding us in the right direction, so we convinced the biker to trust in the guidance it was giving us.

I was relieved to know that I still had the leaf, and I held it up in the air again.

I thought for sure that we were too far away from the hummingbird, but to my surprise the hummingbird came flying up to us and landed on the leaf, saying, "Sometimes helping others can do great things for the soul. Even if you've helped only one person in your life, maybe that person could help someone else. Eventually it could become an epidemic and soon the kindness would spread throughout the world. Just think, it all may have started because of your generosity. Pretty powerful, don't you think?"

The hummingbird flew off and the wind picked up, blowing the leaf to the path on the right. I caught the leaf again and we all agreed to take the path on the right.

CHAPTER 5

Breaking Barriers

As we continued walking the trails, it felt like we were getting closer to reaching the river. Instead of walking uphill like before, now we were heading down the hill. After a time, the mechanic stopped and pointed out something up ahead of us. We all looked through the trees and saw water flowing in the distance.

We ran through the trees and finally found the river at last. We were all ecstatic, but there was still a problem: Just as with the creek earlier, there wasn't a clear path to get to the river. We each took a moment to consider our options.

While we were discussing different ways of getting to the river, a man approached us with a fishing pole in his hand. He told us he was trying to get to the river himself and explained his own challenge in getting there. "With all of the trees and bushes in the way," he said, "we all could be putting ourselves in great danger." He had been contemplating making his own path, but he was a little hesitant because of what could happen along the way.

We briefly exchanged our stories about how we all had arrived at this point and agreed that getting to the river was essential to helping all of us. And we offered our opinions on the best way to do so.

I decided that this was a great time to hold up the leaf again to help us decide on the right path to take. So we told the fisherman the story behind the leaf and I held it up to the breeze.

The hummingbird quickly flew up to us again and landed on the leaf.

The fisherman was amazed—especially when the hummingbird spoke to us.

"Sometimes, when you've finally decided what you really want in life, your path can be blocked. You might have resistance that holds you back. There may be many obstacles to clear, but don't let them discourage you. Don't be afraid to lean on others for support, especially the ones who've been with you from the beginning. You all have amazing talents, so don't be afraid to use them."

With that, the hummingbird flew off and the wind blew the leaf out of my hand. But this time I couldn't catch it. We watched the direction that it blew in, and we agreed to trust in the hummingbird's guidance. Following that advice, we came up with a plan to get to the river.

The biker organized the plan and the mechanic pulled out some tools to help us make a path. The fisherman, with a knowledge of the outdoors, pointed out some of the dangers to watch out for.

We started making our own path to the river and before we knew it, we were already half way there. When one of us got tired, the others worked on the path, so that everyone got a chance to rest. We were almost through the last set of bushes when the fisherman stopped us.

He held a finger to his lips to tell us to be quiet, then he pointed through the trees.

I thought at first that it was the river he was pointing at, but that wasn't what he was showing us. He was pointing to a huge bear that was blocking our path.

We all dropped down low and tried to devise a plan to get past the bear.

The mechanic said that he had the tools to take down the bear if we had to. He was more than willing to take the chance.

The fisherman didn't think that was a smart move given the size of the bear.

The biker thought we could split up and go around the bear.

We all said that there could be other bears close by, so we agreed that sticking together was probably the best move.

I didn't want to hurt the bear, but I was trying to think of a way to distract it if we could. Just then I remembered the sandwich in my bag.

I knew bears love food, so I volunteered to distract it. I told the others,

"I'll lure it away from the path, then you make a run for it."

I navigated my way around to get a little closer to the bear. My plan was to get its attention with the sandwich, then throw the sandwich in the opposite direction. I just hoped that I wasn't going to be the bear's food of choice instead.

I was hiding behind a tree about thirty feet from the bear when it spotted me.

I thought to myself, "Okay, don't panic. Think this through. How far can I throw this sandwich?" I decided I couldn't throw it far enough. But I believed that if I could get the bear going in my direction, then I could lure it away from the others.

I took a few steps away and held up the sandwich. The bear slowly started coming toward me, and I took several more steps away. As I continued taking steps, the bear kept following me. But I made sure to stay a safe distance away from it.

I managed to get about fifty feet away from the others and couldn't see them anymore. But I'd lured the bear far enough away from them and was hoping they were safe.

I saw a clearing through a few trees that looked like a good spot to throw the sandwich. So I let the bear get a little closer, then I threw the sandwich toward the field.

The bear didn't flinch and just stared at me.

"Oh no," I thought to myself. "I think I'm going to be the bear's sandwich."

Just then I felt a buzz by my ear and saw that it was the hummingbird. It looked at me and flew right toward the bear.

I thought the hummingbird was going to be toast, but it was too quick for the bear. After it had successfully distracted the bear, the hummingbird flew toward the field where I had thrown the sandwich. When the bear followed the hummingbird to the field, I took the opportunity to get out of there. I ran back toward the path and the others, who, to my surprise, were still waiting for me.

I asked them why they hadn't made a run for it to the river. They said that they couldn't go through knowing that I wasn't there with them. They also said that we all make our own paths, but together we help each other walk them.

After many attempts to break through barriers, we had finally broken through the last one. We looked out in amazement at the wonderful sight of the river flowing up ahead of us. We each took a moment to appreciate the guidance that the hummingbird provided in getting us this far. After discussing the different messages we had received from the hummingbird, we realized that trusting in ourselves and helping each other had been the key all along.

Chapter 6

Writing Your Path

While we gathered ourselves for our walk to the river, I saw a boat out on the river. Seeing it made me think about an anchor. And the anchor made me think about the importance of having a little support, especially from those who have weathered the storm with you. Suddenly it felt like a huge weight was lifted off my shoulders and things became clearer in my mind.

We slowly walked down to the river, appreciating the beauty all around us. As we walked I noticed that the hummingbird was flying in the wind just above us.

I looked up as the hummingbird shared another message with us.

"Some rivers have been known to possess amazing healing properties within their waters. Some people may be frightened if the water is rough, but if you keep the faith in knowing there's a path to redemption, you can live your lives without the fear of drowning. So be adventurous and go test out the waters."

We made it to the river and each of us took a few steps in to test the water. It was cool and felt wonderful on my feet. Just then the boat that I had seen earlier came closer and stopped right in front of us. The people got out of the boat, and I noticed that they were the same people in the van who we'd helped earlier.

They were quick to point out that what goes around comes around, and they offered up their boat as a gift for our kindness. We tried to turn them down, but they insisted that we keep the boat.

I turned to my three fellow travelers, and they said the boat was meant for me so I could continue my journey.

I looked at all of them and pointed out everything they had done to help all of us get to the river. I told them they were the ones who had contributed the most on our journey; all I did was come along for the ride.

They said that the best way I could honor them was to share the story of our journey in the hopes of inspiring others to help one another. They said I was meant to use the boat to pursue my dream and continue on my path.

I agreed to tell their story and started to get in the boat, but first, each of my companions had something to give me before I set out on my journey.

The fisherman gave me his fishing pole and said, "Never give up on pursuing your dream. I want you to catch the biggest fish in the river."

The biker told me, "There will be all kinds of weather on your journey that will try to slow you down." Then he took off his jacket and gave it to me to keep me warm and dry.

Then the mechanic gave me his advice. "Always keep the faith and keep your positive outlook going sky high." He took a canteen out of his backpack and gave it to me, saying, "Now you have something unbreakable to fill up."

I thanked everyone for helping me get to the river. I promised them I would never forget their generosity. I was very grateful to them for coming with me on my journey, and I was determined to tell our story.

As I stepped into the boat to set off on my journey, the hummingbird came flying up to me again. Only this time it had the leaf.

"Before you embark on your journey, I wanted to return something to you. This leaf is yours and you already know what to do if you need some guidance along the way. I will be more than happy to help you whenever you need me. Now go on your journey and continue chasing your dreams."

I thanked the hummingbird for all the guidance and help along the way. I looked at the back of the leaf and saw there was a message written on it: "Write your own path."

That simple message helped me realize what the next chapter in my life was going to be.

I wasn't proud of the mistake I made that set my journey in motion, but I was grateful I still had choices to make. The mistake wasn't going to control my life anymore. Instead, I was going to learn from it and continue living my dream.

We never know who we will cross paths with in life, but I was grateful that I met the people I did on my journey to the river that day.

I pulled up the anchor and said goodbye to everyone. Then I set sail on the river to continue my journey. While I floated along, I got to thinking about some important things I had learned. So I started writing things down that I thought could help others if they needed it.

There may be many obstacles on your journey to what you want in life. And there will always be people who resist you and knock you down. You may find yourself down in the dirt or cleaning up broken glass. But don't give up hope. There is always a path to picking up the pieces and making yourself whole again. You may need some help along the way, but don't be afraid to accept help or advice from others—especially from those who have supported you throughout your life.

There will come a time when you will know when to pull up the anchor and let yourself be free.

There will always be times when the leaves will fade away and fall, but soon enough they will return and spring back up full of life again.

And most of all, remember this:

Don't be afraid to turn over a new leaf, because you might just find that what you've been searching for was right there on the other side all along.

The world we live in is beautiful. If you don't like the world you see, look within yourself and aspire to be what you want to see. Even a little light can shine for miles in the darkness.

While I was floating down the river I noticed that there was a dragonfly flying along with me. I didn't think too much about it and continued on my way.

But I started noticing the beauty of the dragonfly and just couldn't take my eyes off it. So I started following the dragonfly to see where it was headed.

Although I wasn't sure exactly where it was going, I trusted in my intuition and kept following the dragonfly. Where I was headed next on my journey may be a mystery. But life is filled with many wonderful surprises. Sometimes we can finally learn to relax and enjoy the orchestra setting up right before our eyes.

Wait until you hear about what happens next.

It's going to be a wonderful story.

Author's Special Thanks

I would like to give a special thanks to those who have helped me throughout my journey in writing this story. You all have inspired me to continue living my dream and I thank you all for the support.

The hummingbird: You helped me realize my full potential and encouraged me to continue pursuing my dreams. Thank you for your guidance in pointing me in the right direction. I will always keep in mind the advice you've given me. You are a wonderful person and I appreciate all the amazing things you do for everyone.

To the Anchor: Thank you for standing by me throughout the storms. You have always showed tremendous strength and I'm confident you will get through whatever comes your way. I wish you nothing but the best in life.

To my mom: Thank you for your love and support throughout my life. My passion for writing comes from your love of reading books. I only wish that you could have read my stories, but I know you are still with me helping me write them. Love you Mom.

To my family: I appreciate and thank all of you who have supported me throughout my life. You help me keep that drive going and you make the journey worth it.

To my friends: I have had many friends who encouraged me to pursue things that, had we never met, I probably would never have pursued. Thank you all for being there for me throughout the good times and bad.

There are so many others who have influenced me to continue chasing my dream. Musicians, artists, writers—thank you for the positive messages. Your pursuing your dreams helped me continue chasing mine. Thank you.

To the dragonfly: Although the journey may seem unclear at the moment, I know exactly where my heart leads. Nothing will stop me from pursuing my dream. Love you. ((88))

Author's Special Thanks

To the traveler: If I was going to describe myself in this story, I would say that you could call me the traveler. I've always wanted to see the world and chart undiscovered territories. Through this passion I fully intend to help spread positivity. I hope that it will, one day, lead to peace on earth. I know that our journey always continues, so I will keep you all updated on the next chapter in this journey we call life.

In parting. I would like to thank everyone who has taken the time to read "Turning Over the Leaf." I hope this story can inspire change or help those in their time of need. I believe positivity can be infectious, so don't give up hope. Instead, try to spread it wherever you can. Remember, there's always another path. I hope you all continue chasing your dreams.

I always like to give some advice. Hopefully it can spark a little encouragement in some of you reading this.

If you ever think there is no hope or feel that life as you know it is over for you, always remember this: You have so much love and support around you at all times. Don't be afraid to ask for help from your angels. There is so much love and light within you. Your soul is beautiful, and we were all created with love from the same divine creator. It is a life-changing experience that only you will understand once you see the light. Learning to love yourself first, no matter what the circumstances are, is always the path to finding peace within yourself.

I shine my light for those who struggle, in the hope that they will see their way out of the darkness.

www.ingramcontent.com/pod-product-compliance
Ingram Content Group UK Ltd.
Pitfield, Milton Keynes, MK11 3LW, UK
UKHW040013200726
13854UKWH00001B/182

9 781733 108829